T0104014

# THE
# HAND
— OF —
# GOD

D AVID  P AUL

Order this book online at www.trafford.com
or email orders@trafford.com

Most Trafford titles are also available at major online book retailers.

© Copyright 2016 David Paul.
All rights reserved. No part of this publication may be reproduced, stored in a
retrieval system, or transmitted, in any form or by any means, electronic, mechanical,
photocopying, recording, or otherwise, without the written prior permission of the author.

Print information available on the last page.

ISBN: 978-1-4907-7179-3 (sc)
ISBN: 978-1-4907-7180-9 (hc)
ISBN: 978-1-4907-7178-6 (e)

Library of Congress Control Number: 2016904694

Because of the dynamic nature of the Internet, any web addresses or links contained in
this book may have changed since publication and may no longer be valid. The views
expressed in this work are solely those of the author and do not necessarily reflect the
views of the publisher, and the publisher hereby disclaims any responsibility for them.

Any people depicted in stock imagery provided by Thinkstock are models,
and such images are being used for illustrative purposes only.
Certain stock imagery © Thinkstock.

KJV

Scripture quotations marked KJV are from the Holy Bible, King James Version
(authorized version). First published in 1611. Quoted from the KJV Classic
Reference Bible. Copyright 1983 by the Zondervan Corporation.

*Trafford rev. 03/21/2016*

Trafford
PUBLISHING®   www.trafford.com
North America & international
toll-free: 1 888 232 4444 (USA & Canada)
fax: 812 355 4082

There was a point in my life that I knew God was watching over me, because I love to read Bible stories and pray and did understand it as a child. I also have fear in my life. Fear of darkness was my greatest fear. I had to go sleep with the lights on in my room, because back then, I love scary movies; and these movies used to affect my mind to a point that I really did not want to go to bed. My mother taught us how to pray; the prayer she taught us was "Our Father, who art in heaven, hallowed be thine name. Thy kingdom come. Thy will be done on earth, as it is in heaven. Give us this day our daily bread. And forgive us our debts, as we forgive our debtors. And lead us not into temptation, but deliver us from evil: For thine is the kingdom, and the power, and glory, forever. Amen" (Matt. 6:9–13). That was the prayer my mother taught me. And you know that prayer works because God is an answering God, because He will not leave us or forsake us. His Word will not come back void, but it shall accomplish that which He please, and it shall prosper in the things where God has sent it. My mother told me stories how when we were in Alaska, that when I was a baby, she gave me a bath—I don't know how old I was—but she said when she came to the place where she gave me a bath, I somehow got out of the place, and I went naked outside in the deep snow.

She said when she came back to the room, I was gone. She panicked, not knowing where her baby was, but you know, at that time, God was watching over me, because when she went outside, somehow she found me naked in the snow. God is good! I believe what the Bible says that God is a consuming fire, because in Alaska, the temperature can get as low as fifty below zero outside, but God's heat kept me warm.

There was another time in my life when I was a baby, my mother had birth control pills on a mantelpiece shelf. So my sister and I got those birth controls pills and took them, and we had to be rushed to the hospital to get those pills out of our body. That is why in the book of Jeremiah, it says, "Before I formed thee in the belly I knew thee; . . . and I ordained thee a prophet unto the nations" (Jer. 1:5). Just remember, no matter what your child may do in life, just know that God's hand is over his or her life, because God has the last word. And these are his words, "For I know the thoughts that I think toward you . . . thoughts of peace, and not evil, to give you an expected end."

Many times in life, we abandon those that we feel are not up to our level of skills or intelligence, but when I read the Word, God said He has chosen the foolish things of the world to put to shame the wise, and God has chosen the weak things of the world to put to shame the things that are mighty (1 Cor. 1:27). That's why we don't give up on anyone because we do not know the plans of God for their life. Pray for your loved ones, and then pray now that God will send forth his angels to watch over that baby. That is why I am still here, because of prayer. Even in the times of Moses, Pharaoh sent the forces of his army to kill all the firstborn because he was after Moses, but God protected the baby Moses and kept him from being killed by the enemy, so that says He is the same God today. Just like He did for Moses,

He can do the same for you. All you have to do is put your trust in the Lord, and He will do it for you too because God does not discriminate, but He is God for those who believe in His Word. I know He is real, because I had many terrible things in my life, some are what I did and some are what people have done to me. But I thank God for His mercy because if it wasn't for His mercy and grace, I would not be here today; He gave me second, third, fourth, and ongoing chances to get it right. That is why I must forgive my brothers and sisters the same way God forgave me. I know God is able to do all things. I know that God is able to make all grace abound toward you; always having all sufficiency in all things may have abundance for every good work. In other words, no matter what the condition is, it doesn't matter if you're not smart enough or slow, as people may call you slow or in a handicapped condition, God's grace will much more abound in every situation.

There were times in my life that people used to say I was crazy or slow, but I did not allow that to stop me because I trust in the Greater One, and His name is God Almighty, because He who is in me is greater than He who is in the world. No matter what you go through in life, just know that the Lord will never leave you or forsake. I have received whipping in my life that I thought that I would not make through it, but I know that my mother was just trying to keep me from being a drug dealer or gangster or in the gangs. She loved me enough to chastise me for my wrongness. The Bible says in Proverbs 22:15, "Foolishness is bound in the heart of a child; but the rod of correction shall drive it far from him." Mother raised me in the best way she could; she did not have instructions on how to raise her children but only by the Bible. See, my mother was about thirteen or twelve years old when she felt the power of God. That was when she was in church with her mother;

she hugged a hot potbelly stove, not knowing that she could have been burned or died, but God kept her just as He did with the Hebrew boys when the king Nebuchadnezzar placed them into a burning fiery furnace. Jesus himself protected them, and I believe that's what happened to my mother—that Jesus protected her because she received his spirit.

As time went on, I became a teenager. My heart was full of lust. Because when I was younger, I found a nasty book that was in our house and read and looked at the pictures. And that journey of sexual perversion began in my life so strongly that I was asking God to deliver me from this enemy. My life was turned upside down. I knew that this was a strong spirit because in the Bible, it took down many strong men, like David, Samson, and Israel as a nation, and it caused destruction. My life was a battle with that spirit because each time I felt like I had victory over it, I was drawn back to it. That is why the Bible says marriage is honorable among all, and the bed undefiled, but fornicators and adulterers, God will judge.

For many years, I was crying to God to let me be delivered from that spirit, but that spirit kept playing with me and had me hostage when He wanted to. I remember one night while I was sleeping, I was trying to wake up, but I could not because it felt like something kept my mouth shut. I could not move, so I called on the name Jesus. And when I called on the name, I was able to wake up. Because that demon wanted to kill me in my sleep, but the Word says every knee shall bow to Jesus and every tongue shall confess to God, and I was able to speak. Hallelujah (praise Jehovah)! I know that it was the hand of God in my life, because so many things in life could have taken me. The Bible says in Romans 8:31, "If God be for us, who can be against us?" For there are always trials and tribulations in our life, but know that there is no temptation that has overtaken you except such as is common to man, but God is faithful, who will not allow you to be tempted beyond what you are able to bear. God knows everything that we are bearing—whether we have done it or someone else has done it, He knows. He even knows the number of the strand of our hair. I remembered one day that I wanted in my life. It was a day my cousin got shot twice in the head by a younger man. I was twenty-one years old.

I had an auntie, named Pauline, who used to come by our house and ask me if I wanted to get saved (accept Jesus Christ). I used to tell her I was not ready yet. At that time, I was smoking weed and chasing women. The time she was asking me to get saved and come to the church was also the same time when I got the news that my cousin got shot. So when I heard about it, I asked the Lord to take my life and let my cousin live. Not knowing that if God had responded, I would have been in hell because at that time, I was still in the streets, but it was love that I had for my cousin. I knew he was younger than me, and I and still have time in this life left. But I figured I was older, and it didn't matter for me. All I knew was that I wanted my cousin to live, and I, die. And God did answer my prayer because I became born again and my cousin lived. Hallelujah! I did die in my flesh when I accepted Christ in my life. I died.

Also, a miracle happened for my cousin. He was in the hospital, and they were expecting him to die. So this woman called my auntie; she was someone my cousin knew because my cousin was dating her daughter. So this woman kept on calling my auntie to give her the number of this preacher. My auntie kept making excuses as to why she didn't call this preacher. So one day, my auntie called him, and he said, "I've been waiting." So he told her everything that was about her from childhood until then. So he told her that he would meet her at the hospital.

When she arrived, she was looking for a preacher with a suit on, but he came to the hospital with painted coverall on. So she made a statement and asked, "You're the preacher?"

The Bible says, "Let brotherly love continue. Do not forget to entertain strangers, for by so doing some have unwittingly entertained angels" (Heb. 13:1–2). So this preacher told her to take him to the room that her son was in. The doctor told him no, so he asked the mother the same question, and she said, "I want you to pray his way into heaven," because she did not believe he could live.

So he prayed, and he said to the mother, "Your son is in hell." So the preacher prayed again and said, "Lord, open up his eyes." When he prayed that prayer, my cousin's eyes blinked. He was already off the life-support machine, and the doctor had already written the death certificate. But one thing about the doctor is that he was Jewish, so the preacher prayed a third time and said, "Lord, keep his eyes open this time." So as he spoke those words, my cousin's eyes popped open. The doctor said he did not believe in miracles but he believed now, and so did the mother who watched God raise her son from the dead. That same time, the doctor admitted that he took a piece of his brain from his head. And God grew that brain back in his head, and not only that, but his forehead sunk in, and God brought his forehead back to normal. I praise God for his miracle-working power. They also brought a hospital bed for my cousin because they said he would never walk again, but he is walking today. I said, "Lord, let me die and my cousin live." And God saved the both of us.

After that, or even before that happened, I was living in our house when I heard the news that my cousin got shot somewhere in Detroit, Michigan. I broke out in tears, so I walked down the street, and while I was walking with tears streaming down my face, I saw this man walking toward me. He had a long black coat on, and his face was white and shining. He gave me a Bible tract, and I looked back. After he placed the tract in my hand, he was gone. It was like he disappeared. So I went back home with tears in my eyes, not even thinking about reading the tract. I turned the television on, and had a speaker connected to my TV, an watched movies, but a voice spoke to me and said, "Get the Bible tract that the man gave you." So I picked it up and read it.

Right then, my heart melted, and I felt a change in my life. So I called my auntie Pauline and told her I wanted to get saved and be filled with the Holy Spirit. So that night, she picked me up for evening service for church. It was Bishop Bonner Church called Apostolic Church. I tarried for the Holy Spirit. I was baptized there also. So I was tarrying for the Holy Spirit, with evidence of speaking in tongues according to Mark 16:16–17. The old women were tarrying with me. I thought I had the Holy Spirit speaking in tongues. They said I did not have it yet. So one day, I was in this church with my other auntie, Pat. I was supposed to go to work that night. It was a young preacher preaching that night that if you want God real bad, then you have to let go of some things, and He will come into your life.

I was at that time working at a fast-food restaurant. I was supposed to be at work at that time, but I never got a ride to work that day. It was a Sunday. That night my auntie Pauline picked me up for church. I will never forget the experience I had while in church. They asked for those who wanted to receive the Holy Spirit. So I went up to the altar and tarried for the Holy Ghost. So I kept tarrying and tarrying. It got real late at church. It was twelve or one in the morning when I felt a rushing wind on the altar, and I felt something go out of my hands. See, while I was tarrying for the Holy Ghost, I asked God that I wanted to see people get healed and come out of the clutches of the devils because I did not want to see anyone in bondage. And that's when I felt His presence on the altar. A mighty rushing wind, just like what's said in the book of Acts 2:2, and suddenly there came a sound from heaven as of a rushing mighty wind, and it filled the whole house (but with me, it was the church). While they were sitting, there appeared to them divided tongues of fire. And that's how it was at the altar I was filled with the Spirit of God. I felt so at peace that if the whole world would have blown up, I would not have felt it. There was a power surge so great that when I went home, I left my door open all night, and I did not even know it was open because I was caught up in God's love that He sent his angels down from heaven to guard my house.

Peace in God is real when you had an encounter such as I had when I got saved. Isaiah 26:3 says, "Thou will keep Him in perfect peace, whose mind is stayed on thee: because He trusted in thee." No matter what life throws at you, you can only have peace in Jesus because he is the peacemaker for your life. Know that and stand on it. God is always there when you need him the most. For He says in Hebrews 13:5, "I will never leave thee, nor forsake thee." So trust in Him, and know that He is your protector. He is the provider, the healer, and salvation to those who do not know Him. As time went on, I wanted to tell the world about Jesus, who saved me from my sins, who healed me from cocaine and weed, pills, alcohol, anger, bitterness, and last, sexual perversion with women who were not my wife. The sexual perversion was the biggest of it all, because it had me hooked on pornography and masturbating, which was destroying me and those around me. I cried to God for many years to be delivered from this demon of lust, which was a stronghold in my life. And God delivered me. Now, I no longer walk after that spirit of lust, who had me bound for so many years. I told you in the previous pages of my story how I found a book full of pornography when I was a child, and that journey started there. So I can say today that I am free of it and not looking back. For He had made Him to be sin for us, who knew no sin; that we might be made the righteousness of God in him. Know that God can bring you out of every situation. Now I know the true power of God's love, mercy, and endurance because God has done all these things in my life.

While I was at the car company, a job that God had gave to me, I met this brother named Pat. At that time, Pat was like a young gangster, or thug, so I witnessed to the young brother, and he got saved. But when I was going through my first marriage, Brother Pat was there to ease my hurt and pain through the Word of God. Pat was a brother that when we talked on the phone about the Word of God, I thought that he was reading out of the Bible. When we were talking, he had the Bible in him word for word. I thanked God for sending people in my life to minister his Word to me at a time of weakness because the Bible says, "Brethren, if a man is overtaken in any trespass, you who are spiritual restore such a one in a spirit of gentleness, considering yourself lest you also be tempted." I even thank God for Brother Pat's wife. They both are prayer warriors in the faith. They both came over my house to pray with me when I was going through difficult times. We used to go out in the streets witnessing for Christ. Brother Pat's wife stayed in the car at that time because she was pregnant. So me and Brother Pat hit the streets, praying for people in Highland Park, Michigan. We saw all kinds of miracles, which God's grace had shown on the scene to cast out demons out of people. I remember this one situation when a man was sitting on the corner of a ledge of cement. Me and Brother Pat prayed for the man, and as we were praying, demons came out of the man that he screamed, and as he screamed, this lady came up and asked us what we were doing to her brother because she had never seen brothers from different churches—some Baptist, some Church of God in Christ, some Apostolic, but the one common thing we had was to do the work of Christ and to see the power of God move on people's lives.

We were committed. Even though some of us were going through marriage crisis, we still were committed to share the good news of the Bible. Our hearts were on fire for Jesus because that was all we had, we had nothing left in our lives because our wives had left us. So in order for us not to be burdened in our minds, we held on to Jesus's love, and his love kept us going. The Bible says in Romans 12:2, "Be not conformed to this world: but be ye transformed by the renewing of your mind, that ye may prove what is the good, and acceptable, and perfect will of God." Because we know that our mind is a battleground for the enemy, that is why we should stand on God's Word, and not on our mind but on the mind of Christ.

One day Brother Pat and his wife came over my house, and as they came in, I showed him Jesus's name written on my ceiling. We just started worshipping the Lord and giving him all the praise and glory for that wonderful name. We also witnessed in Detroit on Woolworth Avenue in the front of a food stamp building, telling people how Jesus could save them, and we were witnessing in the cold.

Around February in the '90s, a security guard came out and gave us hot chocolate while we were under the power of Christ. Men were selling and buying food stamps at the same time we were preaching, then they realized that we were preaching the Gospel, and they left that corner, and the food stamp place had closed down because there was so much corruption at that place. So God shut it down. When you know and stand on God's power, He can do anything. We were caught up in the spirit of Christ and nothing else. I remember before I gave my life to Christ, I used to smoke weed, sell, and like to fight, but I never carried a gun because I knew that anger and gun don't mix, but I could use my fist pretty well. I thank God for changing my life so I can be a servant for him and not for myself. For the Bible says, "You were bought at a price. Therefore glorify God in your body and in your spirit which are God's" (1 Corinthians 6:20). I did not know how to glorify God in my body because I was too busy chasing women and trying to fulfill my needs.

That was another part of my life that was challenging. Sexual sin is a stronghold to men and women. It is a destroyer to our homes, churches, businesses that causes men and women to miss God's presence. It seemed like every time I thought I defeated that demon, He rose right back in my life even when I was in the church. There are a lot of people who want to be healed of this spirit of perversion but don't know how. They go to church and read their Bible, and still this spirit takes hold of them. I know 'cause that spirit had me like that. Earlier in the book, I spoke about how when I was young, I looked at that nasty book and that spirit of perversion came on me. Even after I saved, I found out there was something still in my life that I had to overcome, and that was sex.

I understand what the Bible says in Galatians 5:16–17, "I say then: Walk in the Spirit, and you shall not fulfill the lust of the flesh," for there is a war going on between your flesh and your spirit. That was a battle for me, for I was so caught in my flesh that I was picking up prostitutes on the corner and having sex with them in my van. I'm praying every day to be delivered from this demon of lust.

One day I remembered picking up this young lady off the corner, and when I did what I wanted to do to her, I heard the voice of God saying to me, "I brought you out of Egypt into the Promised Land. Do you want to go back to Egypt?" And I said, "No, Lord!" So I said to the young lady, "Let's pray and ask God to forgive us for our sins." We prayed the sinner's prayer that night, and after she prayed, she said she would never go out into the streets again (that she meant she would never sell her body again). So I went on in the power of the Lord again because I had asked for his forgiveness, and He forgave me. Know that God is a forgiving God. There is not one sin greater that He cannot forgive. He alone has the power to forgive. He can clean you up and use you for his glory.

These writings that I wrote awhile back are things I thought I had to beat if these resurface in my life over and over again. I put all these words hoping to help someone out, who is going through the same, so that they can be free. I thanked the Lord God for setting me free from the bondage of perverseness. God showed me that it was like a dog on a long chain, and as soon as that dog ran out as far as He could, the chain would yank him back to the same place, but when you got the key or something that could cut that chain, the dog could run free. That was how it was with me. I would run the race set before me and go so far, then that sexual sin would pull me right back where I was before. So that is why Jesus was the scissors that cut me free from the sexual sin. I thank God every day from freeing me from that bondage that had me, for so many years, tormented. Year after year I was asking God to free me from my sin of sexual addiction. I knew I was free from cocaine, weed, cigarette, alcohol, pills, and sharm, but the biggest part of my life was sexual addiction, which, I can say, I am delivered of today. Thank you, Jesus, for keeping this body!

I also remember when I was separated from my first wife because she wanted another man, I lay on the couch very hurt. See, I never let myself get hurt by anyone, but this one time, I was hurt. I was telling my first wife, "If you come back home, I will forgive you. And leave that man alone." She told me she could not do that. She wanted to hold on to me and the other guy. So the only thing I thought about was the safety of my children. I know my first wife was on drugs, but she would not admit it. So I held on, not knowing what to do, but I did know one thing: that I was not going to share my wife with another man. So I started to go to court so that I could get custody of my children. I had a lawyer, and I knew he was godsent because he did not charge me for taking the case. I waited on my divorce out of 1 Corinthians 7:10–16, and the more I searched, the more I waited, even though I had the right according to Matthew 19:9, which says, "And I say to you, whoever divorces his wife, except for sexual immorality, and marries another, commits adultery; and whoever marries her who divorced commits adultery."

I had counsel with my pastor, who was Pastor McCruthen. At that time, we both came from counseling, and she told my pastor that if I did not act right, she would hold on to the other man. You see, she wanted to hold on to the both of us—to the man she was dating and me. But I know that could not work because God will not allow us to hang on the world and serve him to because He is a jealous God. The book of James 4:4 says, "Adulterers and adulteresses! Do you not know that friendship with the world is enmity with God? Whoever therefore wants to be a friend of the world makes himself an enemy of God. Or do you think that the scripture says in vain, 'The Spirit who dwells in us yearns jealousy?'" So when she said that, I knew it was over because after that, she told me that she was filing for her divorce. I told my lawyer I wanted to get custody of my children.

So when I was trying to get custody of my children, something happened.

The sister of my first wife called me up and started talking. I don't remember the conversation, but it had something to do about my first wife. My children were in the backyard playing. Suddenly, I did not hear my children playing anymore. It was a setup between her sister and my first wife. You see, she drove the car in the alley and took all the children out of the backyard and placed them in her car. At that time, I had no way of knowing that she took the kids, so I asked my next-door neighbor if she saw my children. And she said no. I later found out that she was also part in taking my children. I had to go to work at that. I usually let my sister babysit them at my other sister's house, which was my older sister's. I brought them from her house, and I kept them at my house because my children were young, and they had seen so many wrong things that I could not take it. So I took my children, and the lawyer told me to keep them at my house until the court session was over.

You see, if I was doing things wrong in front of my children, I would want her to take my children from me, but it was the opposite; she was doing wrong in front of my children, and when I asked her boyfriend, he told me that they were doing something in front of the children. So that is why when I picked them up, I kept them.

So going back to the story on how she got the children from me. While going up and down the neighborhood looking for my children, I asked some of the kids who were in the neighborhood, "Have you seen my children?" Some told me that they saw them on the next street, and some said they saw them two blocks down the street. They were playing a cruel trick on me because they also knew what happened to my children. So I thought someone had kidnapped my children. So I called the police and told them what happened, because I was searching frantically for my children. And at the same time, I was getting my ninety days in the car company. So I asked God, "God, I would give everything to see my kids again." And that's when I was driving down 7 Mile going toward the street—that was when I saw my first wife driving down 7 Mile. I sped up to catch her, and she sped away with the children. And then the light changed to red. I pulled the car in front of her and told my kids to come out of the car. God had opened the door to get my children back because He knew that all I wanted to do was raise them up right, because I wanted them to know the Lord and not the world. And when I got them, I told her not to ever come around my way. To say all that, I knew in my heart that I did the right thing.

During the separation, I remembered lying on the couch with tears in my eyes, because I had never ever let anyone hurt me. That is why I didn't get married, because in my eyes, I had seen so many men get abused by their wife. And I said I would never get married, but when I accepted Christ in my life, I wanted to do like the Bible said, "But if they cannot contain, let them marry for it is better to marry than to burn." (He was talking about pleasure.) So that is how I got married. I knew I was hurt, with tears in my eyes, then suddenly something happened. I saw my four children, each of them going down on their knees, praying for me. They were really young. I would say all the way to three years old, praying for their father, and I never told them to pray. They prayed on their own. God was using my children even at that age.

Another time in my life God spoke to me and told me to turn the TV off. I did not listen; I kept watching TV until my children told me they did not want to watch TV and to turn it off. At that time, I had cable in the house. They spoke to me the way that God told me to turn it off. So I called the cable people to come pick up the cable boxes, and they told me they would not be able to pick it up until that next week. So I told them that I would bring it on that day, and they told me there would be a charge. And I told them I did not care. I would bring the box on that day. So right after I turned the TV off, I never knew the talents my children had: my daughter, Jamie, and my son Peter were preaching. And they were ages 4 and 5. They were imitating the pastor at the church, saying things like, "God's going to get you. Quit your fornication! Quit your drinking!" My daughter used to preach that, and my son Peter used to tell my daughter, Jamie, when he was preaching to give him a towel to wipe his face and told her to take up an offering. My son Joseph used to draw pictures. He was seven or eight years of age, and he was selling pictures he drew in the school. My son Hakeem was into basketball. We used to have a crate nailed to the tree where he played basketball. I did not know the gifts my kids had until I turned off the TV. God was showing me something then, but I did not understand it. I was trying to raise my children in the right way, according to the Bible.

When I was still married, I got a letter from my first wife stating a doctor's statement, showing me the medical term of the symptom. It was called craniosynostosis. It is when the bones grow around the brain. So as the brain grows, the bones grow around it. It gives the brain room to grow, but in this case, the brain was growing, but the bones were in fusion (that means they were not moving, so that would cause the brain to have no room to grow), which could cause retardation or other mental challenges. My son at that time was three months old. They wanted to do surgery in his head. What they wanted to do is cut open the head and do some incision, cutting away the bones inside his skull, or cranium, so that the brain could grow freely.

You see, the bones were growing at a slower pace, causing the brain to press against the bones, which caused the head to be elongated (like a water head). So that is why they wanted to do the operation. I was in the navy at that time when I heard the news. I was on the USS *Coral Sea*, an aircraft carrier at that time. I knew this guy on the ship, and he knew the Lord, because when we went to the Philippines, he and others used to spread the Gospel of Jesus Christ. And also, when I had a really bad headache, I walked past him, and my headache was gone. He reminded me of Peter on how they sat the sick in the streets and laid them on beds and couches, that at least the shadow of Peter might overshadow some of them (Acts 5:15–16). So I asked him to pray with me about my son's condition, because my son was at that time three months old, and we prayed together. So later on, a month later (because mail was really slow coming to the ship), my son Joseph did not have to undergo any surgery at all. They took him to two other doctors, and they said he was fine; as a matter of fact, they said he was really smart. So I praised God for healing my son, because if God did not heal my son, he would have been mentally challenged for the rest of his life. So I thanked God for his power to heal my three-month-old son. Glory be to God! Hallelujah, for his healing power.

I also had another son named Hakeem, who was born with a hole in his heart. I used to rush him to the hospital because he was always vomiting after I fed him baby milk. It would not stay in his stomach. He was really skinny; I did not think he would gain any weight. So after church, I took him to the hospital, and they told me to give him Pedialyte. For a long time, I did not see my son with on his body. So I kept praying to the Lord to heal my son. So one day, as he was older, he was trying out for a basketball team, and he had to get a checkup from the doctor to see if he was in shape to play basketball. As they were checking him, they saw something on his records indicating that he had a hole in his heart when he was a child, so they took him to a heart specialist, and when they checked him out, they told me the hole in his heart had closed up. All I could say is *"Thank you, Jesus,"* because Jesus had closed the hole up that was in my son's heart. So he went on and played basketball, and he was good at it. The book of Isaiah 53:5 says, "With his stripes we are healed." And that's what the Lord did for my son. He closed the hole up in my son's heart. God is a healer, but we have to trust in him, and not in men. Me and my children used to witness to the neighbors about Jesus. At that time, I was going through separation because my first wife had left me for another man. The Lord spoke to me when I was lying on the couch and said, "Get up. I want you to go on the avenue and preach my words out there in the park." But I told the Lord that I was hurting, and he said, "Go out. Preach my words." So I said, "Okay, Lord, I will do it."

So as I was preaching in the streets, a man stopped to hear the Gospel of Jesus Christ. He said to me, "I usually do not stop for nobody, but something in you made me stop." So I led him to Jesus, and he gave his life to Christ. And that is when it started for me going out in the streets to be a witness for Jesus. Monday through Friday, I was on that same corner, telling people to get saved, to know Christ, after I dropped my children at school at eight thirty in the morning till the time I had to pick them up at around three o'clock in the afternoon. I used to witness, because God has placed a word in me at the time I lay on the couch in the house. I did not know at that time that it was going to be my calling to evangelize. The more I went into the streets to speak God's Word, the more I forgot about what I was dealing with because Christ became the center of my attention and not my problem. It did not matter anymore because all I knew was that I was geared up to hit the streets to win a soul for Christ. That was the most important thing in my life, winning souls for Christ, not getting money, houses, or cars but see a soul come out of bondage, because the Bible says in Matthew 6:33, "But seek ye first the kingdom of God and his righteous, and all these things shall be added unto you."

At that time, the Lord gave me custody of my four children. The youngest one, I did not get custody of, because my first wife would not let me see my baby for almost three months. So when I went to court for all my children, the judge only gave me the four children and not the fifth, because she said I hadn't seen the baby or was not being in the baby's life—even though she hid her from me these three months. One day while taking my children to school, my first wife was there too, not knowing that I was going to be at the school at the same time, and that was when I saw my fifth child in the stroller. I picked up my daughter and was shouting because I have not seen my daughter in months, saying, "Lord, thank you for letting me see my daughter even though my first wife did not want me to see her." But God made a way for it to happen. My journey of witnessing started then, for the love of Christ and what He did on the cross.

I used to take my children over a brother in the Lord; his name was Aaron. Me, Rokanne, and Kenny used to go over Brother Aaron's house to fellowship. We broke bread together and even took communion together. One day as we took communion, the Spirit of the Lord flowed in that place, and we felt a wind from heaven in the house, and we got on our knees and started praising and speaking in tongues and prophesying. And the Lord met us there because we were on one accord. We were hurting individuals seeking after the power of God in an apartment. I took my children everywhere I went. So they also saw God move in a miraculous way. I wanted my children to know God. I wanted to train them up in a way that when they get old, they will not depart from it (Proverbs 22:6). I did not want them to go the way that I went, but I wanted them to be better than I was. They have seen God's love on people so many times. While we were at Brother Aaron's house, we prayed for the brother who was there. He was hunched up like a cat (I am talking about when it's about to claw at someone or something or when somebody has him cornered, his back goes up as in a fighting position), and that's how this man rose. So we prayed for him. For that was a spirit of lust in him, and we cast that demon out of him. Then he got free, and we started praising God for delivering him from the spirit of lust.

There was another time when me and my children, Brother Aaron, Rokanne, Kenny, and Aaron's cousin was out at night praying for people. One time there was a lady on the street corner, and we asked her if she needed prayer, and she said yes. So as we started praying for her, the police came to see what we were doing. We told the officer that we were leading her to Christ, not knowing who the lady was. The police officer let us pray for the young lady, and we led her to the Lord. And she was changed and surrendered her life to Christ with tears coming from her eyes. Because by us praying for her, we kept her from going to jail, because they wanted to put her in the back of the police car, but God gave her mercy by delivering her soul from hell and also from jail. So we thanked God for allowing us to be at the right place at the right time. The Bible says in Romans 8:14, "For as many as are led by the spirit of God, these are the sons of God." We were hungry to do the will of God because the fire was growing in our souls. He, the Holy Spirit, causes peoples to move in the mighty works of God. And my children experience all that and more of God's glory on the earth. We went house to house preaching the Word of God. We were excited about God, and there was not a boring moment with him.

I remember one time going to the buffet restaurant in Michigan, and that was where we met Donnie. We asked him if he needed prayer, and at that time, he was eating along with some of his friends. He told us, "No, not at this time," but the other guest told us to pray for him, so we prayed, and God blessed that man. Then we went all throughout the day praying for people like the waitresses, the cooks, and others who wanted to be prayed for. We came to a fellowship with one another, but God had something different for us. We ate our meals but could not finish them 'cause our hearts wanted to see someone set free or delivered from the hands of the enemy, because our hearts were full of joy that day. We saw the power of God move up and down through the buffet restaurant. So we praised God for leading us in such a move for him.

One Sunday morning, I was getting my daughter some stockings because she had ripped up the one she had on. While in the grocery store, I did not have all the money to buy the stockings, because at that time, I was a single parent raising four children; my first wife had the other one. The lady in the store saw me trying to buy some stockings and asked me how much I needed, and I told her the amount I needed, and she gave it to me. So in return, I asked if she needed prayer, and she said yes. So I prayed for her right in the store. After I finished praying for her, I got in the line so that I could pay for the stockings and drive to church. I was on my way to church when I noticed a rip on my daughter's stockings. While standing in line, I saw a miracle. I looked back, and this woman was still worshipping God in the same aisle I left from getting the stockings. The glory of God had surrounded her so that she could not move from that spot but give God praise for what He had done in her life, with tears flowing down her eyes. I thanked God for blessing that woman. But it all started with her giving me money to buy my daughter some stockings. And a chain of blessings fell on this woman's life. That's why I praise him and glorify him because He is worthy to be praised and worshipped, not for what He does, but because He is God all by himself. So when I went out the store getting ready to go to my car, the Lord spoke to me and said, "Go over to that car that is parking in the grocery store." And He told me to pray for that elderly lady sitting in the car. So I did as the Lord told me, and I went over there with my kids with me and asked the lady if she needed prayer; she said, "Yes, pray for me." So before I prayed for her, the Lord told me to anoint her. So I told her, "Whatever is paining you, anoint that area."

Two weeks prior to that, I had come from a prayer meeting at the church where Malcom X's bodyguard was a pastor. So they had this one man named Bishop Pate. They called him the oil man and said he was passing out a bottle of oil that he prayed over like the Lord told him to. He was locked up for ten months in a parking shack, and the Lord told him that if he prayed over the oil, wonders would take place. I had that same oil, but I know that it was God's power. I told the woman to put the oil on her. So she anointed her legs with the oil. When her legs were anointed, the Lord told me to tell her to rise and walk. And she got out of the car and walked. The amazing thing about that was, she said, "I have never walked out before for ten years." She had the condition for ten years, and God said in his Word to heal his children.

There was a time when I took my children to the go-cart on 8 Mile and Mount Elliot. They were driving the go-cart; they were a little older then. While we were at that place, something nudged me to go home. So I got the children together to go to the house. On our way to the house, it started to rain. I did not think much of the storm because it was raining, but there was something else about it—the clouds darkened, and it started pouring hard. Imagine, we had not watched TV at all, so we did not know what was happening in the world. We got in the house as fast as we could to get out of the rain. So I got my children in the house, and after that, I went back outside in the rain. Someone would have thought I was crazy to go back outside like that, but I had taken off my socks and shoes and went back outside barefoot. And I was praising God in the rain. While praising God in the rain, I saw a lightning bolt hit the transformer by the corner store, and all the power in our neighborhood went out. There was no power in the neighborhood, and everybody's lights were out. Then I saw another lightning bolt hit that same transformer, and the lights in the neighborhood came back on. The people would have thought Detroit Edison turned the lights on because they came on so quick, but I knew who had turned the lights on; it was not Detroit Edison but God who turned the lights back on, because I had seen it all. Some in the neighborhood did not have light for weeks, but ours came on suddenly. God was that lightning bolt from heaven that turned our power back on, because I was a witness to his glorious power.

And also, there was a tornado out in a part of Michigan that tore it up, but God spared the neighborhood I was in and the other neighborhoods around us, because I believe he covered us with his hands.

There was a time when my son Joseph was sick. I told him if he did not get any better, I was going to take him to the hospital. It was Sunday night. The Lord said, "Pray for him," so I prayed, and after I prayed, he said he wanted to go to church, so I took my children to Sunday evening service for Bible study and church preaching. I thanked God for his voice to speak to me concerning my son. God is always speaking; we just have to listen to his voice. God knew just what we needed in that hour. The scripture says in John 10:1–5, dealing with a thief trying to come to God another way instead of following after the Lord—that is why you need to get familiar with the voice of God and not a stranger's voice (devil), but know the voice of the Lord, and he (God) will work everything out. John 10:3–5 says, "To him the porter openeth; and the sheep hear his voice: and he calleth his own sheep by name, and leadeth them out. And when putted forth his own sheep, he goeth before them, and the sheep follow him: for they know his voice. And a stranger they will not follow, but will flee from him: for they know not the voice of the strangers." That is why I put forth my hands on my son, and God healed him because I heard his voice. I praise you, God, for your magnificent voice. I praise you only, Lord! Glory and honor be unto you alone and not man.

My son Hakeem, at an elementary school in Detroit, used to go around the school, leading children his age to Christ. I remember when he told me that he had led an Arab boy to Christ, that he accepted Jesus Christ as his Lord and Savior. I was proud of my son witnessing at that age in life, because I do not want anyone to die and go to hell but live again in Christ Jesus. These are testimonies that I asked God to help me remember so that I could put them on paper to exalt His name, to show that if you just put your trust in God, He can bring you out of every situation. But too many times, we trust in our own devices, strategies, and smartness, and we fall every time. But with God, there are no failures but only victories in Christ Jesus, for He is the only one who can save us in this world. Even when you are faced with lies about you, God can bring you out.

I know that to be true, because I was faced with a lie concerning my daughter.

Some individuals accused me of things about my daughter. She was about to be five years old. I went through, but God kept my mind in the midst of it. I had to go through child protection service because they came over. When the lady came over, she told me about the situation that was said about me that someone told her, but she said something else to me. And I know it was from God. She said it was only a test. She said, "Don't worry. God will bring you through." So I told the other person about it, knowing that it would be my fate. And when I told this person what the other person told me, she called the police for me, because these two people knew each other; it was all about the money. By getting custody of my daughter, they were going to split the money that they would get from the State for taking care of her. The State never took my daughter from me because they did not have proof about the matter, but I was tormented by them. But I stood on God's Word that he would never leave me or forsake me. (It is so sad that a lot of men are locked up in prison for a lie, because someone wants to get back at them, so they use the child to hurt the individual even to a point of death.) I know because I was that person who was lied upon even to the point of death. The police called me and told me to come to the police station, so when I got there, I explained to them that I did not do what the individual said that I did to my daughter, and I told them that I was willing to take a lie-detector test concerning my daughter. So they told me they would give me one. I said okay.

They called me up a week later and told me to come in and take the test. And when I was going to take the test, they sent me to the officer or the detective. I do not remember what his title was, but they called him the preacher. When I took the first test, I passed, but when I took the second one, I failed. So he told me that all I had to do was confess that I did it and they would get me some help concerning it. But I told him I did not do it to my little girl, so he told me that I must have been like David, who was in the Bible, who looked at Bathsheba while she was bathing in the tower; and I told him I did not do it to my daughter. He then told me I must be one of the guys taking children in my van, and I told him I was not that person. He was trying to connect me to an unsolved case that they had not yet solved. You know the sad part about that was, there were people who did the crimes but had not been caught. They caught one individual and blamed all the other crimes on that individual so that they could quiet the people. And what they were trying to do to me was get me to confess something I did not do and blame me for other cases that they did not solve. So after I told him that I did not do it, he stormed out the door mad because he wanted me to confess and say, "Yes, I did it," which I did not do. There were so many people who had confessed to a crime that they did not do because of the police scare tactics or promise of how they were going to help them out, which were all lies told to just get that person to confess things that they did not do. That was the case with me. The other police officer, a lady, told me that I better not leave town and also told me to call the police station every day. They said if I missed calling them anytime, they would lock me up. So I started calling the station every day at a certain time to let them know that I was still in town. So the Lord spoke to me and said, "Give them Bible scriptures every time you call." So I started giving them scriptures like, "I am more than a conquer through Jesus Christ," "I walk by faith and not by sight," and "I can do all things through Christ who strengthens me." These are some of the scriptures in the Bible I was quoting every time I called them.

I quoted so many Bible verses every day until they did not want me to call them anymore. I thanked God for bringing me out of the fire. They also had the attorney general who was supposed to get in contact with me also, but he never even called me. I praise God for his victory over the enemy. Even when I was in Southwest Detroit, a guy pulled a gun, but not pointed at me, holding it alongside of him, and this was before I took a lie-detector test. An individual told someone in their neighborhood that I molested my daughter. While I was praying for my daughter, I heard someone say, "Shut up," and I replied that I feared no one but God. I and my three sons were going to the car (that was the second incident dealing with being threatened), and as we got in the van, I saw two guys walk up to my van; one guy had a sawed-off shotgun in his hand.

The guy came up to me and said, "I heard you molested your daughter."

I told him I didn't. I love my children and would not do any such thing to her.

My son yelled out, "My father didn't do nothin' like that!"

I told him that I took a lie-detector test to prove my innocence.

And then the man told my sons, "If he messes with you, let me know."

That's when my son yelled out and said, "My father did not do that!"

I told the guy, "Jesus loves you, and I love you too."

Right then his countenance changed. That was when he told me to get out of Southwest Detroit and not to come back, but I told him I couldn't do that, because I had two daughters that I visited. So I left after that and went home, but before that happened, my daughter was already taken away from me by my wife's boyfriend.

I will never forget that day. It was the day a friend of mine from my old job, the car company in Detroit, came by my house and brought me Easter baskets (at that time I still had my daughter). He and his wife surprised me when they came over. They had all types of baskets for my four children. At that time, my baby daughter was not with me, for her mother had kept her. All this happened on a Saturday. The next day I was taking my kids to church. I dropped over their mother's house on Friday and was going to pick them up Saturday night. At that time, I got on my knees, praying like I usually did, but I saw a vision while praying. And in my vision, I saw my little girl taken from me, and I shouted, "No, Lord, don't let her be taken from me!" with tears in my eyes seeing all this in a vision. At that time, I got off my knees, getting ready to pick my children up from their mother's house, but at that time, I was short of cash. I needed some gas to put in my car. I called up one of my aunties and asked her if she had any money; she replied yes. So I went over her house to pick up the money. It was about 10:00 or 11:00 p.m., so I got the money and went to a gas station to fill the tank up, and at that time, I saw an older lady there too, so I asked her if she wanted to receive Christ into her life, and she said yes. So I prayed for her, and she received Jesus Christ as her Lord and Savior. So I proceeded driving to pick the children up over to their mother's house.

When I got to the house, I saw my three boys coming out of the house, but I did not see my little girl. So I asked where she was.

My wife and her boyfriend replied, "She is not coming."

I kept saying, "Bring my daughter out!"

The man proceeded and reached through his pocket. I saw some guys across the house, and I asked one of them if I could use his phone. He said yes, and I started calling the police and explained to them what happened.

Then at that time, another guy came out and said to the guy on the porch. "You let that pervert use your phone. He molested his daughter."

Right then, I heard one guy say, "Let's beat him," and another said, "Let us shoot him," and another said, "Let's stab him," and I told my three sons, "Let's pray." My sons were really young at that time. We prayed, and right as I was praying, I heard someone say, "This man went crazy," because it was around two in the morning, and we were still praying. (The police never showed up). But I believed that God dispatched his angels to the place we were at, because when I had finished praying, the whole neighborhood was clear. There was not a soul outside. The whole street was cleared. (You see, this neighborhood was active all night and all day.) God sent his angels from heaven, and they formed a shield around me and my boys.

The scriptures say in Psalms 103:19–20, "The Lord has established his throne in heaven, and his kingdom rules over all. Bless the Lord, you his angles who excel in strength, who do his Word, heeding the voice of his word." That is why I know without a doubt that God sent his angels to fight off these demons that wanted to attack me, and I thanked God for fighting my battle. After that, the man who stayed downstairs from my ex-wife's house came out to my car and started to say hateful words to me, but his girlfriend came out and said, "Leave that preacher alone. He did not do anything." So he went back to the house after she said that. She did not know me, so when she said preacher, it was by the Holy Ghost. I thanked

God for his goodness and mercy upon me. Even though the police never showed up, God sent his angels, and they showed up to rescue me. Before all this happened, I was at the church house preaching the Word of God. The lady in whose house I preached at decided to buy my children some Easter clothes. She was an older woman who worked with me at the car company. She asked her husband if it was all right to buy some clothes for my children, and he said yes. So she bought dresses, suits, shoes, and socks so that they could look nice on Sunday, and also, when I was with the childcare worker, she told me it was only a test. Knowing this, I found that it was still hard to go through all this for one lie, because someone was greedy and let the devil use him. She had spent over four hundred dollars on all my children's outfits, which was a blessing, because all I was trying to do was raise them on the Word of God so that they would teach the same Word to their children.

I went back home without my daughter, and it was hard, but I kept the faith. I kept trusting in the Lord. In the Bible, it says, "Trust in the Lord with all thy heart, and lean not to thy own understanding. In all thy ways acknowledge Him, and He shall direct thy paths" (Proverbs 3:5–7). All this that was against me, God's hand was still greater in my life. Even though there were mishaps on my part, He was still greater. It taught me how to depend on God more than my own wisdom, because He knows every hair that is on my head. And He is the King of Glory; no matter what comes in my life, He is still faithful.

I remember before I went through dealing with lies about my daughter or before I got married, I was a young seventeen-year-old going into the navy. I asked my mother if she was okay with me going into the service, but at that time, they had a delayed program, where, if my mother approved me going in, all I had to do was take my test to be a navy man. She approved my request to go into the service. So I took the test, and I barely passed by one point. I know it was God. He allowed me to pass the test, and I did. God was guiding my footsteps; I was not yet saved, but I loved to pray. Even as a kid, I loved to pray and read different stories out of the Bible, like Samson and Delilah and other stories. I was hearing about the book of Revelation, for my cousin Samuel used to read that book to me. It scared me because it talked about the long teeth in Revelations 9:7–8. On their heads were crowns like gold, and their faces were like the faces of man. And they had hair like that of a woman, and their teeth were like those of a lion. Those were seeds that were planted in my life as a kid.

I remember being in Virginia and going to a FRAMP school to know how to help out a pilot, like chocking the plane, putting ejection seat pins, and other things. After finishing schooling, they sent me to California. It was warm, and it was my permanent station where I was going to be at during my service time in the navy.

While I was on base, I met a friend of mine who was in Virginia with me at school, so we started celebrating with beer, liquor, and weed. (This was before I was saved). We were celebrating in our barracks. They ran out of liquor and beer, so we decided to go to the store. We walked to the store because it was right outside of the base, and going there took about twenty minutes or so. While we were at the store, some friends of mine were talking to a white lady; this was in 1980. So I came out of the store and saw it. While talking to the white lady, the other girl told him, "Get away from her, you nigger." He slapped the one who said that, because there were two girls at that time.

She went into the club that was next to the store, and when she went in and told them in the club, a whole bunch of white people came out chasing us, saying, "Stop those niggers! Stop those niggers!"

The guy who hit the girl traded coats with me. I did not thought about it until they knocked me down, and the woman said that I was the one who slapped her. But I kept on saying that I did not do it. There were a lot of people standing around me like in a circle when I realized were I was at. They were waking me up with smelling salts at the base. I believe when the other guys found me, they carried me to the base. And the people who jumped on me probably thought that I was dead. And I believe after that, they walked away from me, leaving me there. I knew *again* that, even when I was not saved, God watched over me, because despite all those people who were around me, I did not have a mark on my face. Only a tooth got knocked out of my mouth. My face was not even swollen. And I knew again that it was the angels of the Most High God who protected me. After going through that, I wanted to get back at every white person, but I remembered one of the guys in the service with me. He told me that everybody did not do that to me. So after getting into fights with white people and trying to hurt them in the military for what had happened to me, I forgave them because of that one statement (not everyone did that to you). It broke the spirit of hatred out of me.

There was another time when I was in the Philippines, because the aircraft carrier I was on pulled in a city in the islands. When I got off the ship, I was looking for a woman to be with. There was a girl in the Philippines. We were off the base in the city. I was young at that time. So I went over to her hut. In the jungles, huts were made from tree limbs. I rode in a two-seater basket with the motorcycle attached to it. So right after we had a relationship, I looked on my neck, and my gold chain was gone. So I asked for my gold chain. I said, "Give me my chain." She said she did not have it, which I knew was a lie, so I started shaking her, asking where my gold chain was. When I did that, she took a machete that was lying on the table and said, "You tried to kill me. I will kill you." (I was not trying to kill her; I just wanted to get my chain back). I don't know how I got outside of her house while the lady was swinging the machete back and forth at me, but all I know was that the same pedicab (a cart hooked up to the motorcycle) came to that same house. It was a different person. It reminded me of Lot when God sent His angels to rescue Lot because he was going to send fire and brimstones on Sodom and Gomorrah. God saved him because he was Abraham's nephew, the same way with me, because of my mother's prayers. Even when I was not saved, God sent an angel in the form of a pedicab driver to pick me up at that woman's house. I knew it was God's angel, because there was no phone to call a driver, and also, *I was in the middle of a jungle.* All I know is that the woman continued to wave the machete at me back and forth. I was also arguing with the pedicab driver, telling him I would give him one peso, and he kept saying two pesos. As the lady got closer to the pedicab that I was in, I told him I would give him two pesos (in which one peso was equal to a quarter, and two pesos was equal to fifty cents). So I was about to lose my life for not giving the driver fifty cents. As I told the driver that I was going to give him two pesos, he drove off at the same time the woman was trying to cut me inside the pedicab. I thanked God even for His mercy, because I could have been dead out there in that jungle and no one would have known anything about it. This lady was out to cut me up if she could, but God rescued me. Thank you, Lord!

There was another time when I was on the aircraft carrier. I was working on the aircraft engine at that time on the flight deck (a place where the aircrafts are launched off the ship). I was on the USS *Enterprise* at that time when a yellow shirt (those that guide the aircraft to be launched) turned the plane on me, because the ship was turning and, at the same time, the yellow shirt was turning the plane too, telling the pilot to put more Thrush out. I was right where he was turning the plane, and the Thrush hit me. I was holding on to this ped-iye (where chains are tied down to so that the plane won't move) for my dear life, because I saw the toolbox that I was working out of go right into the ocean. So I praised God that He did not let me burn up or get blown off the deck into the ocean.

God is a good God, a merciful God, a holy and faithful God who keeps his Word concerning his promises. And all these times I was not saved, but He watched over me until I accepted him. You have to know God for yourself; nobody else can know Him like you do. He is personal to them who want to get close to Him, because he is love. All the experiences I had showed me how much God loves me, even when I did not have that personal relationship with him. It's not how much God does for us, but how much we do for God, and all he asked of us is to believe His Word. His words will not change because he is God. And forever He will not leave us or forsake us. We may leave Him, but He will never leave us.

I remember the time when Brother Rokanne and I went up to Mount Clements, Michigan, on an assignment for the Lord. We met a man on a corner, and we asked if he needed prayer, and he said yes. So we started praying for him. While we were praying, I looked up, and the people were standing outside their doors outside the porch, because while we were praying, God shook the whole neighborhood. Everyone came out of their porch at the same.

And I heard this man say as he opened his door, "What was that?" Then he said, "It surely feels good."

It reminded me of Paul and Silas when they were put in prison, and as they gave praises to God, God shook the prison so hard that all the prison doors flew open. That is what happened that day in Michigan. Everyone came out of their house at the same time.

Then another time, we saw a man in a wheelchair on his porch. So we asked him if he wanted prayer, and he said yes. Also, we proceeded to pray for him (for he was in that wheelchair for over a year, never being able to get out of it). So we continued praying. All of a sudden, the power of God moved on him, and he started to get out of the chair, but his grandson came out and said, "What are you doing to my granddaddy?" When he said that, the man fell back on his chair and did not get his miracle. So he fell back on his wheelchair, and we left just because the grandson did not understand. Matthew 9:18 and also Luke 8:41–55 deal with Jairus's daughter when she was dead. Jesus told them that she only slept, and they ridiculed him, knowing she was dead. But He put them all outside, took the girl by the hand, and called her, saying, "Little girl, arise." You stand on God's Word believing that it shall come to pass.

I also remember this woman who was in the store purchasing something. We asked her if she needed prayer, and she said yes, so we started praying for her in the store. There was me and Brother Rokanne, and as we prayed for her, we saw God change her countenance to the point that she looked new. So as I was going out of the store, she prayed for me, and I fell to the ground. After that, people gathered all around me because they thought that I might be hurt from hitting the cement ground like I did. Brother Rokanne was out there with me. Someone said to call the ambulance, but Brother Rokanne said he was all right. He was just slain in the spirit, and also the woman who got saved in the store started preaching and telling people, who were gathered around me, to accept Christ as their Savior and to put away their sins and believe in Jesus Christ. This woman was preaching with fire, and some of the other people were listening and receiving Christ. I felt the power of the Holy Ghost when she laid her hands on my head. This was the same woman who was in the store who got prayed for and then turned around and laid hands on me. The power of God is great, because He knew just what we needed at that time. I love the Lord because He first loves me. He knows all about our struggles, our downfalls, and our pain. He knows them all. He is a better physician than a doctor, because when He heals you, you are completely healed, not temporarily but completely healed of all sickness and pain.

Doing the will of God is what kept me in perfect peace. Isaiah 26:3–4 says, "Thou will keep him in perfect peace, whose mind is stayed on thee: because He trusteth in thee." God is so good because He kept my mind so many times when I could have lost it all. These are journeys that I experienced with God. He is my father; He corrects me when I do wrong and takes me back to the straight and narrow road. I know because I felt His love and His strength when I was all alone and when I was weak. Even when everyone walks away from you, He is still there. God's love is genuine; He doesn't hate you today and then hold on to your past as some do, but He forgives you as you forgive others, and that is the kind of God I serve.

When I work for a car company in Detroit, there was a friend of mine who told me about R. W. Shamback, who was in town on 7 Mile and State Fair Street. He told me I ought to go see him. I went to the tent service, and there were so many people there from the city looking for a miracle for their life. So I took my four children with me to see him (at that time my youngest daughter was with her mother). I saw God use this man in a miraculous way. One time I saw a woman in a wheelchair, and he prayed for her, anointing her with oil out of a big barrelful of oil. And she got up out of the wheelchair and walked.

And another time I saw a man on crutches walking to get prayed for, and he got healed. He dropped his crutches and walked. I too was looking for some type of miracle in my life, but as he prayed for me, nothing happened, I thought, but as I was walking away after he prayed for me, a white man, who had holes in his blue jeans showing his knees, with a red handkerchief tied around his head, started speaking to me. At that time after Shamback prayed for me, I started speaking in tongues profusely. As I was speaking in tongues, he did not say I was going to interpret the tongues; he just started speaking, saying to me, "You see this tent?"

And I said, "Yes, Lord. Yes, Lord."

He said, "God is going to give you ten times the size of this tent.

"God said you love to travel. He is going to have you travel all over the world preaching his Gospel.

"Demons will try to kill you, but God's angels will be with you.

"You see the people in this tent?"

I said, "Yes, Lord. Yes, Lord."

He said, "God said He is going to give you a hundred times more in this tent."

After he said all that, he was gone. So I looked around for that man to tell him thank you for that prophecy, and he was gone like he had disappeared out of thin air.

I asked my children if they saw the man I was talking to, and they said, "Dad, we did not see any man." (But they were right beside me.) And I asked another person if they saw the man, and they said no also. So I believed that God had sent a messenger from heaven to tell me of the things that would happen in my life. No one saw the man I was talking to, and all the time that he was speaking about what God said about me, I was speaking in tongues.

I remember years ago, a guy called my house looking for someone named Tiffany. I knew I had a niece named Tiffany. So I wanted to find out why he was calling my number. I asked him, "What do you want with Tiffany?" He told me that they were having a baby, but he found out that the baby was not his and that she cheated on him. He told me he wanted to kill her, so I told him let us pray, and he prayed with me. And as we prayed, another voice came out of him that was demonic. It was like praying for two persons when there was only one person I was praying for. I started praying because I thought it was my niece he was talking about, but I found later that was a different Tiffany, not my niece. After we prayed, he gave his life to the Lord. And after that, the one he was looking for called to my house too. Her name was Tiffany, and she was looking for the one I just prayed for. I told her what had just happened when I talked to her boyfriend, and she got quiet for a moment. And I asked her if she wanted to accept Jesus as her Lord and Savior, and she said yes. So I prayed with her also, and she accepted Christ. God knows all, because he intervened against the devil's plan for both their lives, because two people accepted Jesus. What the enemy meant for evil, God turned it for good. Thank you, Lord, for intercepting the enemy's plan for their lives. I could have said, "You got the wrong number," and this young Tiffany could have been dead. But God had me pray for the man as well as the woman. God worked out for them both because they both accepted him. God is holy and righteous; he is also all-knowing because He knows the number of the hair on our head. That is just the God we serve.

There was a time in my neighborhood when a house caught on fire. It was the middle house. That was between my neighbor and the first house closest to the corner. As the house burned, its fire reached the first house on the corner, and then it spread to my neighbor's house. I was trying to help her put out the fire, but we did not have enough water pressure. At that time the fire department came. And when they used the fire hydrant, it did not work because in the summertime, the children had turned it on and used the water up to cool themselves down from the heat. So the fire truck had to hook it up to another hydrant, and as they were doing that, the blaze got bigger and bigger. The fire department people told me not to go back into my house. But I heard the lady who stayed next door to me on the opposite side say, "Lord, don't let my house burn down." The other lady's house had burned down even though they were putting water on the house. As the flames were going toward my house, my son looked up at the flames and saw a wind push the flames away from my house back to my neighbor's house that was burning. When he said that, I looked and saw it too. All because my neighbor spoke out and said, "Lord, don't let my house burn." God heard her cry. Her house never got burned with the fire that was spreading, and my house didn't either. But little bits of shingles were melted because of the heat of the fire, and that was the only thing that was touched. God spared both of our homes. There was always prayer going on in the house, because that was all I knew since I was a child till I was a grown-up, even when I was not saved (accepting Jesus as my Lord and Savior).

I prayed a lot. One time me and Brother Rokanne and Aaron went over to this lady's house. She was an older lady from a Baptist church, and she had a daughter who was in a wheelchair. We prayed for her daughter, and she got out of the wheelchair and started walking. When her mother saw that, she was the precious gift of the Holy Ghost, and she received Him in her belly and started talking in tongues (fiery tongues). Then around two weeks later, she passed away. She received the Holy Ghost, and God took her home. We started praising God for her daughter and her mother being filled with the Holy Ghost, not knowing that she would pass away later on. The old folks used to say, "He is on time," because God will never leave us or forsake us. He said, "Ask, and it shall be given you; seek, and you shall find; and knock, and the door shall be opened" (Matthew 7:7). God will never fail you. God has placed the anointing on all my children because when they were firstborn, I prayed for each of my children and said to God, "These are yours. Use them for your glory." I know because one day I did not have a job; I was getting unemployment, because my job at the car company had laid me off indefinitely, but I wanted to work. So my youngest son, Peter, said, "Dad, you are going to get a job today." I told my son I received it. I went to the gas company to pay my bill, but I left my bill at home. So I had to fill out a slip so I could pay it. While I was filling out the slip, a security guard came over to me (notice I did not know the man), and he asked me if I knew somebody in the church who needed a job. I looked around and said me. As I got in line waiting to pay my bill, he came up to me again and said someone was on the phone and wanted to talk to me, and he also said, "Don't worry about your place in the line." He said he would place me back in my spot. He gave me the phone, and I talked to the guy. He asked me when I could start; I said today, but I had to get a babysitter for my children because at that time I was raising them on my own. So he told me okay, that I could start today. He said, "Come whenever you get a babysitter." And I said okay. So my stepsister volunteered to watch over them, and I started working that day. My son was really young, but what came out of his mouth was God's Word, and I believed it. The Bible says out of the mouth of babes and suckling comes perfect praise. And also death and life is in the power of the tongue—either we can receive death or life from the words we speak (Proverbs 18:21). The man who hired me told me to just go to the job, and when I got there, to tell them who sent me, and they would have me working. The job paid five dollars an hour, but I wanted to work. And God blessed me, and I paid tithes out of my check and paid a car note that was 448 dollars a month. At that time, my car-note payments were way above my head, but I believe God was behind what the car dealer told me—that every note should be met and that it would be paid off.

While I was working for the car company, I was making good money at that time back in September 1995. I went through a divorce with my first wife, and after that, I came back to work because I had taken a day off for my divorce. I came back to work the next day looking for my time card so that I could punch in. They told me to go to the office, so I went to the office. And then someone told me to go back to the line, so I went back to the line. At that time, they told me that I was definitely laid off (meaning that I did not know when I would get a callback). When they told me that, I lifted up my hands and started praising the Lord. They thought I went crazy, because I said hallelujah real loud, got my papers, and walked out the door. That is why I bought a van, and I also had a car, but when I came off a fast food and looked outside, somebody had stolen my car. But my next-door neighbor said that she saw me riding in a van. So when I bought a van, she was shocked. That is why even when I had this five–dollar-an-hour job, I held on to that word that all my car notes would be met. When I missed a car note, they sent a tow truck to take away my car.

I know that because when I got home, I had a note in my door saying, "We came to pick up your van, but you were not at home." At that time, I called my own car company and told them my situation. And they asked me how much I could put on it, and I said about one hundred dollars. So they told me to pay 120 dollars a month until I caught up with my payment. Then after that, the company I worked for called me back to work. And I was able to pay on my car note again. Even before I got hired back at my car financing company, they gave me extensions on my car note. That is why I know without a doubt that God will supply all your needs according to his riches and glory in Christ Jesus. And when I got laid off again, they sent me a check for 2,400 dollars, and I paid off my van. I did not know that I was getting money from the car company, but what I found was, they had a small retirement stock fund put aside for the employees, which I knew nothing about until the check came in the mailbox. All you have to do is trust God's Word for He cannot fail. The Bible speaks about God trying to find someone to swear to, and He could not find anyone, so He had to swear to Himself. God had spoken to me again, and this time while I was praying, the Lord told me to go to the city airport to work. I thought that I would work as an aircraft mechanic because I was certified, but He had me do something different, like drive a fuel truck. So I went to the city airport, me and my children for the job. When I got there, a security guard told me that they were not hiring for any job. So I walked away, and then I heard a voice say, "Did I tell you to go?" And I said, "Yes, Lord." So I asked the security guard if I could just visit the place, and she said yes. I went in the small terminal where the pilots lodge was at and asked the lady at the front desk if they were hiring, and she said no. So I walked away out of the terminal heading back to my car. And as I was walking, I heard a voice say, "I will get you in for work." He asked me if I had any kind of document, such as a résumé. I said yes, and I gave it to him. The Lord showed me that in two days, I would be hired for work. And two days later, they called me to come to work. I took a urine analysis test for drugs and was hired two days later.

At that time miracles started happening. The man who got me in renewed his vows with God. He spoke in tongues and spoke revelation and knowledge on the Songs of Solomon. O how God had great love for his people. We both wept being in the presence of God concerning that scripture, and others got saved too. God's fire was surrounding the city airport. Many times I had to fuel at the gas station the cars for the pilots to drive. I had time to pray for those people, and God spoke in their lives about things that they knew only God knew. People got delivered right at the gas station.

Then one day, while fueling the truck—I was on top of the truck to fuel it—I felt the presence of God, and I started to dance for the Lord. I said, "No, Lord, not up here in a comical way." Because the truck was long and high so you could see a long way down. And that was when he spoke to me. God told me to go to the car company.

He said, "I have some who knew me and left me, and I want you to bring them back." I heard the voice of God audibly. It was like someone speaking to you in your mind. After hearing his voice, it took two years before I started working back at the car company. I worked at the city airport about a year and a half before getting a call telling me I could go back to the car company. This time when I was called back, we had Bible studies with almost forty or more people. They were lined up against the conveyor belt when we were preaching Jesus. One lady got so convinced by the Word that she said she would never go back to the casino, and another person got delivered. We had church on the job, and God blessed us.

Before going back to the car company, while I was still working at the city airport, after God spoke that word for me to go to the car company, I went home and noticed someone had broken into my house. Not one time but four times in one week. And each time they broke in, I boarded up the door. And every time they broke in my house, they stole things like a toolbox (a rollaway toolbox), other things, and a phone. Also, when I was going to an employment office to apply for the car company, I met a friend of mine named Norm. I did not have a babysitter, so I asked my sister (the oldest) if she would babysit, and she told me no. So I took my children with me to the employment office to apply for the company. When I got there, the side where I was supposed to apply at was closing, so I told the lady that someone was expecting me. And when I said that, the person came out and said, "Yes, I am expecting him. Come right on in the office."

They let me bring my children in with me. He gave me a card to take to the examiner so that I could take my test. I asked that person who gave me the card to pray for me. And he prayed and said, "You got the job." I knew everything was divine, because when I took the peg test (moving pegs from one hole to another), everybody's clock was working except mine. I knew in my heart I did not do good the first time, but God allowed the clock not to work in order for me to get a greater score on my test. So they told me to retake the test, and I passed with high scores. I had to go to the next level in which a group participated in solving a problem in the work area. At that time, my brakes went out, and I did not have enough money to get them fixed. I needed a babysitter again for the children, but I asked my sister again, and she told me no. So my friend Norman said yes, he would watch them.

While I was driving, they taught me what to do was shift my gear to one to slow down my car because I did not have brakes. So I did, and it slowed down the van so that I was able to park it. After that, I got my brakes fixed. The next step was to take my physical examination. I drove to the place trying to get directions on how to get there. I knew some of the directions, but I did not know how to get to the clinic. So I asked this one guy on how to get there, and he gave me the directions. And as I was driving, I was supposed to make a turn on one street, but I made the wrong turn and ended being right back on the freeway. As I was driving to get off the freeway, my transmission went out. Imagine, that was a 1997 Voyager, and it was 1998 at that time. I only had an hour before I could take my physical examination, because I always tried to be there early when I had a long way to drive. So I told God if it was for me to be at the car company, let it be, but if not, let it not be (that was what I told God). See, no way humanly possible that I would be able to take my physical examination within an hour, with a van broke down on the freeway and transmission fluid all over the freeway. But God heard my prayer, because the next thing I knew, a white lady stopped and said, "How can I help?"

And I told her, "Do you have any transmission fluid?"

She said no, and I said thank you. And she drove off.

Then another man asked me, "How can I help you?"

And I told him my van broke and I needed transmission fluid. He told me that he was an owner of a tow trucking business, and he told me he would send a driver to me. So I waited, looking at my watch to see how much time I had to be there at the clinic. After I looked at my watch, the truck was there to take my van to the clinic. I gave him some money, and he dropped my van at the clinic, with me in his truck. And he gave me a card saying when I got finished with my physical examination, I should give him a call to take me and my van back home. When I got to the clinic, I threw my hands up and started praising God for his goodness and mercy. At that time in my life, I trusted and believed God, but at that time, I did not know because here I had a situation where my vehicle broke down and I was way out somewhere with no way to make it to my destination. That was what I thought, but I prayed that if it was God's will, then his will be done, and God showed me that it was his will for me to be there. I thanked God because Satan thought he had stopped me, but God was directing me in every step of the way. The scripture says in Psalm 37:23, "The steps of a good man are ordered by the Lord: and delighteth in his way." God greatly delight when we allow him to order our steps, and He pours out on us in a mighty way.

I remember that Saturday when the car company called me to come to work in August of 1999. But the part that was a miracle was, I had a phone that my sister gave to me that she knew did not work, but she gave it to me anyway. And this was during the time that they kept breaking in my house. They broke in my house four times in one week, and I found out who did it. Because the girlfriend of the man who broke in my house said she was on the lookout person at that time. This was the same lady I took to church, and her children used to go with me too. But they did not stay with her because they were taken from her and were given to her mother. Every time they broke in my house, they took some things and my telephone. So I brought another telephone, and they did the same thing again. I got mad and took off from work, parking my car around the corner, and I cut off all the lights in the house, waiting on them with a wooden bat in my hands while I was sitting on a chair.

I said to myself I was going to get there, but I heard the voice of the Lord telling me to turn those lights on and park my car in front of my house. (God knows what's best for me because it could have gotten worse than that.) So I did what God said. And I say again, the phone that my oldest sister gave me did not work at all. When she called my house, the phone rang, and she asked how did the phone ring if it didn't work. It was on a Friday when she said that, but that Saturday morning, the company called me and said that that was my luckiest day, but I told them this was my blessed day. And they told me to report to work, and that was the next day, after talking to my sister about her phone. God's promises are yeah and amen. I started witnessing at the company, and people were getting saved by the power of God. While at the company, the Lord spoke to me and said, "Tell the people to get ready for a famine, but he also said it was going to be like Joseph's time." When I was telling them that, they all ignored me, thinking that I was crazy, but I kept warning the people. And when I got transferred to another department, I warned them too, but they also thought I was crazy. I spoke that word from 1999 to 2007, and that was when we went through bankruptcy, because at that time, the people were making so much money along with profit-sharing checks that they did not care about the warning. I told them for eight years straight that God spoke to me to tell them to get ready for a famine. And when that famine came to the car company in a form of a bankruptcy, many people took the buyout (giving them a lump sum of money, and that was it, no retirement pay or benefits). So many took the buyout before they shut down the plant. Someone asked me if I was taking the buyout, and I told them no, because I was standing on God's Word. And when Obama bailed out the auto industry, I knew God's Word had come to pass. And it was not man, it was God, because at first, they were not going to bail us out, but they saw the ripple effect all over the world, and that was when they helped out the automobile. Proverb 21:1 says, "The king's heart is in the hand of the Lord, like the rivers of waters; he turns it wherever he wishes." And that was what He did to the president. God is in control of everything because heaven is His throne and the earth is his footstool. And after the bankruptcy, I saw people coming from different states, because their plant was shut down, to come to our place to work.

The same thing God showed me back in 1999 came to pass in 2007. And then he spoke to me again, "Tell those same people who did not believe the prophecy about the company going into a famine." After that, they believed. God allowed us to have a prayer room at the company; it was done by the UAW and the company negotiations. They allowed us to have church right in that room. We had Bible studies, and we preached the Gospel from Monday to Friday on our break time at 10:00 a.m. to 10:30 a.m. God moved mightily at the plant. People got saved, delivered, and even some spoke in tongues. Some became ministers, pastors, and deacons—all in the little room we preached in. We even had revival where there were over thirty people hearing the Gospel of Jesus Christ, and most of all, we were from different religious sects, but we were unified in our beliefs in Jesus.

I remembered when God told me to stay in the temple, so every day during all my three breaks, I went to that room and prayed, seeking the face of God. Of what I was going through, I knew that God had the answer to my problem. I did that for five or six years, staying in that prayer room on the three breaks on my job. I saw cancer destroyed, the dead come back to life, marriages healed, all kinds of miracles on the job, because God commissioned me to go to the car company and preach the

Gospel of Jesus Christ. I went through two bad marriages, but I had to still keep the faith. I remember God giving me a Word, saying, "Greater days are ahead of you." But when I looked at my situation concerning my second marriage, I could not see it, but I kept going to the house of the Lord, going to prayer from 6:00 p.m. to 9:00 p.m. every Friday. I did not miss a bit concerning God's temple because I knew that there was refuge in the house of the Lord. I thanked God for Pastor McCruthen and Bishop A. D. Knight, who both taught me to be the man of God that I am today.

It reminds me how Eli took little Samuel under his wing until God prepared Samuel to be a priest and a prophet, or better yet, Paul ministering to Timothy, telling him to stir up the gifts in his life. After all that, God gave me a wife; it was nothing that I chose, but God chose for me. He gave me a prophecy about her on April 30, 2007, and I did not know at that time that she was going to be my wife. The prophecy says, "Write these things down, my son, that what I have is holy, my servant. I choose her to be your wife, for I am holy, my servant, and that what I choose for you is holy. Many gifts shall come your way. Even when the enemy comes, my Word says yes to you both. Know that what I, the Lord, put together, let no man put asunder for I am God. Gifts shall come from the east, north, west, and south. You shall stay holy in my temple daily. My divine plan is on your life. Stay in my word. Prophesy and speak what I say and say what I speak. Know that I, the Lord God, speaks that houses shall come, finances shall come, clothing shall come, cars shall come. For you have favor in your life. For that which I, the Lord, have put together is holy unto me. Know my words, son of man. Know my heart. Keep my words holy as I am holy in you. Know that I joined you and your wife together. Ponder no longer." This was the prophecy that God gave me when I was at a certain place in Michigan, Wednesday, at 9:06 a.m., while praying to God. These are the testimonies that God did in my life. Whether I was messed up or not, God did not forget his promises toward me. I thanked the Lord God for not taking his hands off me, because if He did, I would have been in hell right now, but He didn't. He loved me in spite of me. (Revelations 12:11 says, "And they overcame him by the blood of the Lamb and by the word of their testimony, and they loved not their lives unto the death.") And that is what God has done for me, and He can do the same for you. Just pray this prayer with me, "Lord Jesus, forgive me for all of my sins. Wash me in your [Jesus] blood. Cleanse me from all unrighteousness. I believe that you [Jesus] died on the cross and were buried on the third day and God raised Him from the dead. Right now, Lord Jesus, I open the door of my heart and make you [Jesus] my Lord and Savior."

Now by praying this prayer, ask, where is the Lord Jesus? Your response is, "He is in my heart." Once you know that He is in your heart, you can now know that greater is He who is in you than he who is in the world. Now when you receive Him, you are saved, and that's according to 1 John 4:4. Now after that, ask God to baptize you in His (God) Spirit, according to the book of Acts 1:8 and Acts 2:1–4.

This is the story that God had me write down. Be blessed, all of you. And one more thing that I want to say is, the beautiful woman whom God gave me is Mary Elizabeth. We are going nine years of marriage in 2016. God bless you. What God has for you is for you.

Printed in the United States
By Bookmasters